A Note to Pc

DK READERS is a compelling program for beginning readers, designed in conjunction with leading literacy experts, including Dr. Linda Gambrell, Director of the School of Education at Clemson University. Dr. Gambrell has served on the Board of Directors of the International Reading Association and as President of the National Reading Conference.

Beautiful illustrations and superb full-color photographs combine with engaging, easy-to-read stories to offer a fresh approach to each subject in the series. Each DK READER is guaranteed to capture a child's interest while developing his or her reading skills, general knowledge, and love of reading.

The four levels of DK READERS are aimed at different reading abilities, enabling you to choose the books that are exactly right for your child:

Level 1 – Beginning to read
Level 2 – Beginning to read alone
Level 3 – Reading alone
Level 4 – Proficient readers

The "normal" age at which a child begins to read can be anywhere from three to eight years old, so these levels are only a general guideline.

No matter which level you select, you can be sure that you are helping your child learn to read, then read to learn!

LONDON, NEW YORK, MUNICH,
MELBOURNE, and DELHI

Art Editor Jane Horne
Senior Art Editor Cheryl Telfer
Series Editor Deborah Lock
US Editor Adrienne Betz
DTP Designer Almudena Diaz
Production Shivani Pandey
Picture Researcher Jo Haddon
DK Picture Researcher Sally Hamilton
Jacket Designer Chris Drew
Illustrator Paul Weston
Indexer Lynn Bresler

Reading Consultant
Dr. Linda Gambrell, Ph.D.

Whale Consultant
William Rossiter, Cetacean Society International

First American Edition, 2002
04 05 06 10 9 8 7 6 5
Published in the United States by DK Publishing, Inc.
375 Hudson Street, New York, New York 10014

Published in Great Britain by Dorling Kindersley Limited.

Library of Congress Cataloging-in-Publication Data
Jenner, Caryn. 1963-
    Journey of a Humpback Whale / written by Caryn Jenner.
    --1st American ed.
      p. cm. -- (Dorling Kindersley readers)
    Summary: Follows a humpback whale as he swims from the
Caribbean Sea to the far north of the Atlantic Ocean.
    ISBN 0-7894-8514-1 -- ISBN 0-7894-8515-X (pbk.)
    1. Whales--Juvenile literature. [1. Humpback whale. 2.
Whales.] I. Title. II. Series.
QL737.C424 J426 2002
599.5'25--dc21   2001032600

Color reproduction by Colourscan, Singapore
Printed and bound in China by L Rex Printing Co., Ltd.

The publisher would like to thank the following for their kind permission to
reproduce their images: c=center, a=above, b=below, l=left, r=right.
Cetacean Society International: William Rossiter 2tc, 2ca, 5clb, 14-15,
16ca, 16bc, 17, 18br, 24, 25br, 29; **J Michael Williamson Photo/Whalenet
(www.whale.wheelock.edu)**: 5crb, 7br, 26-27; **Bryan and Cherry
Alexander Photography**: B&C Alexander 21; **Bruce Coleman Ltd**: Jim
Watt 9, 12, 33br; Pacific Stock front cover, 4tc, 10tc; **Corbis**: Peter
Johnson 27tr; **Environmental Images**: Roger Grace 21tr; **FLPA - Images
of Nature**: Brake/Sunset 6-7; F Nicklin/Minden Pictures 15tr; R
Pitman/Earthviews 32cla; **Salvatore Siciliano**: Salvatore Siciliano 22-23;
Still Pictures: Ray Pfortner 32cr; **Corbis Stock Market**: Craig Tuttle 10br;
Amos Nachoum 19; **Telegraph Colour Library**: Peter Scoones 2bc, 30-31.
    All other images © Dorling Kindersley.
    For further information see: www. dkimages.com

see our complete product line at

www.dk.com

 READERS

BEGINNING
2
TO READ ALONE

Journey of a Humpback Whale

Written by Caryn Jenner

DK Publishing, Inc.

SPLASH!

SPLASH!
A humpback whale jumps
out of the sea.
He is named Triton (TRY-tun)
after a sea god in ancient myths.

Triton has a very powerful tail.
The fins at the end of his tail
are called "flukes."
Triton has special markings
under his flukes.
Every humpback whale
has different markings.
Do the flukes of these humpbacks
look different to you?

Triton's flukes

Whales live in the sea,
but they are not fish.
Triton breathes air like humans
and other mammals.
He can hold his breath under water
for about 30 minutes,
but usually he swims to the surface
every 4 to 10 minutes.

Then Triton breathes through
the blow-holes at the top of his head.
He sprays a cloud of mist into the sky!

Blow-holes

Humpback whales
have two blow-holes.
The mist from a whale
is like your misty
breath in cold weather.

blow-holes

Sometimes Triton makes
special noises under the water.
GROAN–GRUNT–CHIRP!
Triton sings loudly,
repeating the same song
again and again.
The eerie sounds of his song
can be heard far away.
Only male humpback whales
like Triton sing the special song.
He sings so other whales
will know where he is,
especially female whales.

GROOOAAN GRUNT

CHIRP

Triton has spent the winter
in the warm water
of the Caribbean Sea.
Now he is hungry.
There isn't much food
for a whale here.

Warm water
In winter, whales
swim to warm
water to mate
and to give birth
to their young.

It is time for Triton to swim
thousands of miles home to the
far north of the Atlantic Ocean.
He lives there for most of the year.
The water is cold in the north
and Triton knows that it will be
full of good food to eat.

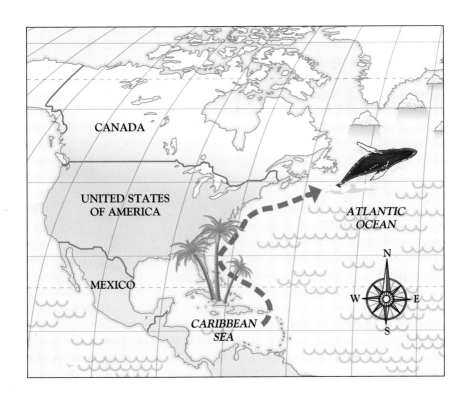

SWISH, SWISH!

Triton moves his mighty tail
up and down as he swims.
He uses his long flippers to steer.
His skin is smooth and sleek
so he can glide through the water.

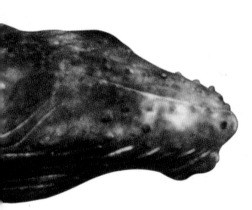

Triton swims at a
slow, steady pace.
He has a long
way to go.

Swimming
Whales, dolphins, and
porpoises move their tails
up and down to swim.
Fish move their tails
from side to side.

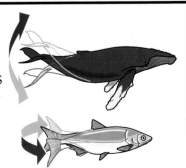

Triton meets his friend, Spoon,
as he swims north.
They travel together for a while,
playing as they swim.
Triton and Spoon poke their heads
out of the water and look around.

Eyes underwater

A clear layer of film covers a whale's eyeballs. This protects the whale's eyes from the sting of the salty sea water.

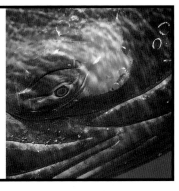

Triton listens carefully.

He can hear many sounds

that help him to know

what is in the ocean around him.

Now he hears a loud SPLASH!

What is it?

It is Spoon.

She leaps out of the water

in a move called a "breach."

Now it's Triton's turn.

He dives backwards with his flippers

high in the air.

SPLASH!

After all that swimming and playing,
Triton and Spoon take a rest.
But Triton is only half asleep.

Part of his brain must stay awake to
remind him to swim to the surface
and take a breath of air.

A mother whale called Salt
swims nearby with her calf.
This is the calf's first journey north.
She learns to swim and dive
by watching her mother.
As she grows, the calf will develop
a layer of fat called "blubber",
which will give her energy
when food is hard to find.
Blubber will also keep her warm
in cold water.

First breath

Sometimes, a mother whale helps her calf to the surface to take its first breath of air.

Triton dives under the water,
and swims north.
Look out!
It's too late.
Triton is caught in a fishing net.
He rolls around and around,
trying to escape.
He has been underwater too long.
He must swim to the surface
to breathe.
SWISH goes his mighty tail. SWISH!
Finally, Triton finds an opening
in the net and swims through
to the surface of the water.
At last, he opens his blow-holes
and breathes the air.

Dangerous nets

Many whales and
dolphins die when
they are accidentally
caught in nets or
other fishing gear.

Triton feels weak, too weak to swim.
He drifts with the ocean tide
and it carries him to the shore.
Triton can feel the sandy seabed
scrape against the skin on his belly.
He must swim back to deep water,
or he'll be stranded
on the beach.

He tries to swish his tail.
Bit by bit, he moves backwards,
away from the shore.
His strength is coming back.
SWISH. SWISH. SWISH!

As he swims north,

Triton hears the sound of a boat

in the distance.

It is a whale-watching boat.

The people on the boat

gaze at him in wonder.

This makes Triton feel much better.

He knows they won't hurt him.

Triton swims toward the boat.

He breaches and flicks his tail.

The people laugh and take pictures.

Whale-watching
Whale-watching
boats leave from
many coastal
places, depending
on the season.

Food for whales

Humpback whales feed on small fish such as sardines, herring, and tiny, shrimp-like creatures called "krill."

Triton swims farther north,

where the water is colder.

He takes a giant gulp of cold water.

It is filled with many small fish.

Instead of teeth, Triton has

long bristles called "baleen."

He filters out the extra water

through the baleen,

then swallows the fish.

Delicious!

Whales gather wherever
there is enough food.
Soon Triton sees his friend, Spoon.
Together, they dive under the water,
blowing bubbles in a big circle
to catch a school of herring.
Triton surfaces,
his mouth full of fish.
SKREEK! SKREEK!
Hungry seagulls arrive to see if
Triton will share his catch.
He lets them have a few fish.
Triton is almost home,
where there will be
plenty of food for him
and many other whales.

SKREEK!

SKREEK!

SKREEK!

At last, Triton arrives home!
It has taken him 35 days.
He swam nearly 2,000 miles
from the Caribbean Sea
to the cold waters
off the coast of Canada.

Now Triton will stay here,
swimming and playing,
and eating as much fish
as he wants.
Then, when winter comes again,
he will make the long journey south.

SAVE THE WHALES

Humbacks like Triton are only one kind of whale. There are other kinds of whales, too, like the giant blue whale, and the square-headed sperm whale. They all need our help to survive.

Many whales have been killed by hunters on whaling ships. Whaling is now against the law in most of the world, but whales are still in danger.

Fishing equipment, such as nets and traps, is one of the main dangers to whales and dolphins. Luckily, Triton escaped from the fishing net, but it left scars on his skin.

Pollution is extremely harmful to whales. Imagine gulping down a mouthful of chemicals and other garbage along with your fish. It could be deadly.

Help to protect whales and other sea creatures by cleaning litter off the beaches. Cleaner beaches make for cleaner oceans.

To find out more about whales, how to help them,
and where to go whale-watching, contact:
Cetacean* Society International, P.O. Box 953, Georgetown, CT, 06829
www.csiwhalesalive.org

To find out more about saving the Earth's natural resources,
including whales and other animals contact:
Greenpeace USA, Suite 300, 702 H Street NW, Washington, D.C., 20001
www.greenpeaceusa.org

*"Cetacean" [seh TAY shin] is the scientific word for whales, dolphins, and porpoises.